Stretch and Pray

Stretch and Pray

A Daily Discipline
for Physical and
Spiritual Wellness

Murray D. Finck

Augsburg Books
MINNEAPOLIS

STRETCH AND PRAY
A Daily Discipline for Physical and Spiritual Wellness

Large-quantity purchases or custom editions of this book are available at a discount from the publisher. For more information, contact the sales department at Augsburg Fortress, Publishers, 800-328-4648, or write to: Sales Director, Augsburg Fortress, Publishers, P. O. Box 1209, Minneapolis, MN 55440-1209.

Scripture quotations, unless otherwise noted, are from the New Revised Standard Version Bible copyright © 1989 by the Division of Christian Education of the National Council of the Churches of Christ in the USA and used by permission.

Scripture quotations marked NIV are from the Holy Bible, New International Version, Inclusive Language Edition, copyright © 1973, 1978, 1984 International Bible Society. Used by permission of Zondervan Publishing House. All rights reserved.

Cover design by Laurie Ingram; cover photo © Julia Toy/Stone/Getty Images. Used by permission. Unless otherwise noted, all photography by Leo Kim Photography, Minneapolis.
Book design by Michelle L. N. Cook

Special thanks to Rachel Lynn for supervising the poses during our photo session and for modeling section one. Thanks also to our other models: section two, Shereen Askalani; section three, Chad Jackson; and section four, Rebecca Anderson. Erin Finck and Anne Finck are pictured on pages viii, x, and xix; these photos were taken by Murray Finck.

Royalties from the sale of this book will be contributed to the ELCA Hunger Relief and the Stand with Africa campaign.

Library of Congress Cataloging-in-Publication Data
Finck, Murray D., 1949-
  Stretch and pray : a daily discipline for physical and spiritual wellness / Murray D. Finck.
    p. cm.
  ISBN 0-8066-5137-7 (covered wire-o bound : alk. paper)
  1. Stretching exercises. 2. Prayer—Christianity. 3. Spiritual healing. I. Title.

  RA781.63.F54 2005
  613.7'182—dc22   2004028826

Printed in Canada

09   08   07   06   05   1   2   3   4   5   6   7   8   9   10

To Rhoda,

my encourager and companion

in my daily pilgrimage

C o n t e n t s

Acknowledgments

I am thankful to the following persons for their assistance, support, and inspiration:

My companion and spouse, Rhoda, and my children, Erin, Anne, and Adam, as they gave me permission to claim sacred space in the early morning hours for time of quiet and centering. Erin and Anne kindly posed for postures in an early version of this resource, and are shown in the front section of this book.

Roy and Carol Oswald, for teaching me a way to begin the day that changed my life and my prayers.

The people of the Pacifica Synod who have gathered in early morning hours with me over the years and continued to ask for this resource as a teaching tool for their ongoing health and wholeness routines.

The staff of the Pacifica Synod as they assisted in the produc tion of this book in a variety of capacities.

Most of all, I am thankful to God for meeting me in the early morning and then throughout the day in my joys and in my pains, always with abundant hope and care, and loving embrace.

A Word from the Author

I began this routine in February 1998, while taking a four-week mini-sabbatical with my friend, the Rev. Roy Oswald, and eleven other pilgrims. Roy, an Alban Institute Consultant and the CEO of Life Structures Resources, planned and led the pilgrimage. We traveled to Thailand and hiked the highlands northeast of Chang Mai, enjoying the hospitality of the Karin hill tribe people there. Our pilgrimage took us on to Nepal, where we trekked an ambitious part of the Annapurna Loop of the Himalayan Mountain Range. Each day, we began early in the morning, quietly, devotionally, using a series of stretches, aerobic exercises, and postures to prepare us for the long day's trek. We ended this morning routine in a circle and prayed over the day, petitioning God's presence on the journey before us, upholding one another and interceding for our loved ones left behind.

I was forty-eight when I joined this adventure. I had wanted to accompany Roy Oswald since first hearing of his pilgrimages five years before. There was one thing that caused me concern about this journey, especially as the day for departure neared. For the previous twenty years I had endured chronic back problems from an injury I sustained at the age of twenty-eight. Now, in my late forties, my life and work was such that I spent many hours a day either behind a desk, driving the crowded and often slow freeways of Southern California, or sitting in airplanes and airports. I suffered varying levels of back pain on a daily basis. Relief was only temporary from over-the-counter pain relievers and many trips to medical professionals.

During those twenty years, I had been under the care of an orthopedic surgeon and had done all the physical therapy he prescribed. I attempted many different cures, all of which were only slightly helpful. The discomfort and pain always quickly returned. As one who loves the outdoors—hiking, backpacking, river rafting, and other forms of activity—I was deeply disappointed in the reality that at age forty-eight, this lower back pain had taken a significant toll on my entire system for the past twenty years.

My health was not improving, and even managing it was not working as well as I had hoped. It was, in fact, getting worse, as I began to experience bouts of sciatic pain that moved up and down my legs.

From the first time I heard Roy Oswald talk about the biannual pilgrimages he led to exotic, far away places, I longed to join one of his trekking trips. After missing several opportunities, and in spite of my back problems, I decided to sign up with him for a pilgrimage in 1998.

For months prior to the trek, I did as much physical exercise as possible in preparation for the demands of this experience. I lost some weight and built stamina through exercise. I was alarmed, however, that the more I physically prepared, the more my back pains increased. Adamant that I would not cancel my registration, I began regularly visiting a chiropractor, who sometimes scheduled me for three days a week, often twice a day. We were trying everything possible to find some lasting relief from this chronic pain.

With no real relief, and still dealing with the daily ache, I left for Thailand and Nepal, apprehensive but determined not to lose this opportunity. I was very uncertain of what this long, challenging journey was about to offer.

On the first day our small group was together, we began as I earlier described. It would be part of our daily preparation for this spiritual and physical pilgrimage into the remote regions of those two magnificent countries. Using a variety of movements and postures each morning, some of which are described in this book, we prepared ourselves for the daily journeys afoot that were to take us from eight to fourteen miles a day, at varying altitudes, some as high as fourteen thousand feet above sea level.

Toward the end of the first week of the pilgrimage, I awoke in my tent one morning without the usual dull pain that normally settled into my system over the night. I lay quietly, waiting for its return. I waited to feel it sharpen as the day unfolded. The pain did not come that day, and it has never returned. I have not had a backache since that early day in our pilgrimage to Thailand and Nepal. I celebrate this new freedom from pain and give thanks to God for the healing and health that I have experienced after those long twenty years of suffering.

I cannot promise the same for anyone else. I only share my experience and offer the testimony of my own personal experience. It has made a significant impact on my life during these years since 1998.

As regularly as possible—normally each early morning—I stretch, exercise, and pray. When I am with any group within the church body I serve, I invite them to join me. We have stretched and prayed early in the mornings at our Synod Assemblies; at the Pacifica Synod Women of the ELCA Conventions; at our Professional Leaders' Conference; at retreats with pastors, deans, and staff; and even at a churchwide assembly.

I have recorded the routine I use in this book. Along with a brief description of each posture, the reader will find a Bible passage. These offer a place to begin one's prayerful meditation. For many, it would be challenging to focus on all of these thoughts and passages in one daily routine. In the back of the book, one will also find journal pages with a devotional thought. One might choose to reflect upon one thought each day and record your experience. There are thirty-one reflections and passages of Holy Scripture, one for each day of the month.

As you move through these physical and spiritual exercises, it is my hope that you will take time each day to thoroughly enjoy one inspiring thought from this discipline and allow that reflection to help shape your day.

Carve out a regular time for exercise. For many people, a daily discipline for a shorter period of time proves to be more helpful than a longer, once-a-week session. The routine I use takes about thirty-five minutes. I prefer the early morning while there is still little or no light.

Create a welcoming environment. Find a quiet place with as few distractions as possible. A carpeted floor will be more comfortable than harder surfaces. You may wish to use an exercise mat or pad or even a large towel for the prone or seated postures. Wear comfortable clothing that does not restrict your movements. I make myself comfortable in a dimly lit part of the living room, and I light a single candle to remind me of the light of Christ that brings the dawn and hope of yet another new day.

Select your music. If you enjoy background music during your routine, it's best to use something that reaches into your own being. Considering mixing a tape or CD with a variety of your favorite selections. Choose music that will center you, inspire you, and guide you through the discipline. The music I use is a collection of pieces that have some meaning for me and assist me in these quiet disciplines for the body and soul. My selections come from a variety of sources—folk music from Nepal; "O Lord, Hear our Prayer" from the music of Taizé; a piece from Marty Haugen's "Evening Prayer;" and finally, "Veni, Sancto Spiritus" again from the Taizé community. These recordings are easily found through the Internet or in many religious bookstores.

As an alternative to creating your own recording, you may consider purchasing tapes already assembled for these types of exercises. The Rev. Roy Oswald has a collection offered through the Life Structure Resources catalog, which can be accessed on the Internet at *www.lifestructure.org/catalog.htm*. Under the section titled "Holistic Quest," you will find six different cassette tapes that may be ordered individually or as a set. They are listed as resources for "pursuing your journey to physical, spiritual, and emotional health."

Consider length and regularity. If you create your own music tape or CD, time your music selections to match your schedule and routine. Using the same music regularly helps you stay on course through the discipline. Within a short time, you will begin to match your movements to the music and no longer rely on this resource to guide you.

Customize your routine. The particular stretches and postures offered in this book are suggestions for a series of movements that I either learned or developed while preparing for and participating in fairly rigorous outdoor activity. Maintaining these disciplines helps my overall fitness. Your needs may be different. Some of the stretches might be omitted, extended, or changed to better serve your purpose. Adapting the routine to fit your own needs is always recommended, especially if you have physical complications. You may wish to check these movements with your doctor to ensure they are appropriate for you.

Helpful Hints before You Begin

Be patient and intentional. This routine offers no "quick solution" or "fix." Instead, it is a set of disciplines for a brief time of centering the day on holistic health and wellness, and on prayer and meditation. Setting aside twenty to thirty-five minutes each day (or more or less as time allows) to engage in these centering movements and prayers demands very little and offers much as a refreshing and energizing way to embrace the day.

To support the meditation and prayer benefits of your routine, I have included a section with a variety of prayer forms and postures, including moments of adoration, confession, receiving absolution, petition, intercession, and contemplation. I have suggested devotional thoughts and verses you may choose to contemplate while doing the movements. You may wish to focus on just one thought and verse each day.

Consider setting a theme for your day . . . especially if you do the routine each morning. One word or phrase is enough. Write the word or phrase down and leave it in a place to which you will return at the end of the day. You might wish to use the journal pages for recording these thoughts. During the quiet of your stretching, your reflection, your prayers, and other devotional time, think about this theme. Throughout the day, allow the theme to guide you. At the end of the day, as part of your evening meditation, disciplines, and prayer, further reflect on how that theme guided your activities.

Tailor your routine . . . to meet your available time, your level of comfort, even your space. Make it completely yours, so that you look forward to this time rather than seeing it as an obligation, duty, or chore. Attempt to make it a daily activity in a time and space that allows you to either begin, end, or pull away from the stresses of the day and from outside distractions. Allow it to become a gift for you each time you stretch and pray.

And most important . . .

Start slowly and take care. Do not do anything that hurts. It is not the purpose of this routine to strain any part of the body. This routine is simply to loosen and strengthen the muscles, ligaments, tendons, and joints on a daily basis. Listen very carefully to your body, how each part is feeling, how it wants to move, whether it is at or past its limit. Only stretch or move within your comfort level. Allow your body to flow quietly and intentionally, in rhythmic, meditative and prayerful ways, without harsh or forceful motions that stress any part of the body.

If you are concerned about a position, or if your doctor advises you that a suggested stretch is not helpful or healthy for you, do not use that movement in your routine. Omit it, substitute another stretch, or hold other positions for longer durations.

Over time, and in very small increments, you may wish to move to new levels of longer stretches and further extensions. With regular discipline, the various parts of the body will normally move and stretch increasingly as they gradually grow stronger and become more toned.

Breathe deeply. Intentional breathing is an important part of each exercise. It is a helpful, healthy, and holistic discipline. Draw in deep, full breaths, filling the lungs to capacity. Exhale just as deeply, cleansing the lungs. Exhaling through slightly pressed lips creates some back pressure and helps to more fully exchange the air in the lungs. Breathing "out loud" during this stretch and pray routine is most acceptable, even recommended. Allow your inhalation to be a time of receiving the gifts of God. Offer a brief prayer as you exhale.

The suggestions in this book are intended to move and stretch a variety of muscles, ligaments, tendons, and joints, and to do so without straining or overexerting any part of the body. For some, a regular routine has provided more flexibility and toning of the body. It also provides a spiritually nurturing discipline for times of centering and prayer. However, these postures and movements may not be helpful for all. Use caution and discernment before beginning any new physical routine.

Disclaimer and Caution

While holding certification in spiritual development and formation, I have not had any formalized training in physical fitness or physical exercise. The initial learnings of this suggested routine came from my involvement with a small group of people preparing daily for the exhilarating experience of trekking the hills and mountains of Thailand and Nepal. It was the "wake-up call" for the day, preparing body, mind, and soul for each segment of this somewhat rigorous pilgrimage on foot through highlands and mountain ranges. From that simple daily routine, I have expanded the stretching and prayer movements to those appearing in this book. This book is intended as an offering to others who wish to develop their own routine of toning body and soul for the journey of the day.

I cannot assume responsibility or liability for another's use or practice of these stretching motions and movements. Decide what will be beneficial for you and for your body and follow your decision. Consult your physician if you have specific concerns or questions about any of the motions.

Following this or a similar routine will be experienced differently from one person to the next. What works for me may not be beneficial for you. Take ownership and responsibility for the disciplines you set for yourself and practice them with joy. Choose carefully the parts of the stretches that you believe will be helpful. Start slowly, cautiously. Customize the routine to fit your needs. Listen very carefully to your body. Do only that which energizes or uplifts you physically and spiritually.

The Movements

Section One:
On Your Feet

You may wish to light a candle as you open your daily routine.

Stand up straight with feet slightly apart, arms at your side.
- Take a deep breath. As you inhale, raise your arms to the side and then overhead. Clasp your right wrist with your left hand and stretch your arms upward, reaching for the sky or ceiling. Keep your right hand and fingers straight.

Option: As you feel comfortable, slowly raise yourself upward by standing on the balls of your feet. Achieve balance by shifting your arms.

- As you exhale, release your wrist. Slowly and intentionally, allow your arms to fall to your side as you lower yourself onto your heels.
- Breathe in deeply. Exhale completely.

Repeat the entire stretch again, this time taking hold of your left wrist with your right hand.

●   ●   ●

Let us lift up our hearts as well as our hands to God in heaven.
—Lamentations 3:41

Stand up straight with feet slightly more than shoulder-width apart, arms relaxed at your side.

- As you inhale, lean to the left, bringing your right arm up to the side, palm up, and then over your head.
- Allow your left hand to rest on your leg for balance.
- Lean to the left as far as you are able.
- Hold that posture.

Option: As you are comfortable, look up at your right hand.

- Slowly exhale as you return to the upright position.
- Breathe in deeply. Exhale completely.

Repeat this movement, this time slowly leaning toward the right, bringing your left hand over your head.

● ● ●

To you, O LORD, I lift up my soul.
—Psalm 25:1

Stand up straight with feet slightly apart.
- Hold both arms in front of you, fingers pointed upward, elbows bent at a right angle. Place your left elbow in the crook of your right arm.
- Turn your left palm to face the same direction as your right palm. Using your right hand, take hold of your left thumb.
- As you take a deep breath, use your left arm to pull upward as far as you are able.
- As you exhale, use your right arm to pull down as far as you are able.
- Repeat the up and down movements one more time.
- Release your arms gently, allowing them to swing freely.
- Breathe in deeply. Exhale completely.

Repeat this movement, this time with the right elbow inside the left.

She girds herself with strength, and makes her arms strong.
—Proverbs 31:17

On Your Feet

On Your Back

On Your Stomach

Six Postures of Prayer

Group Movement

Journal Pages

Stand up straight with feet slightly apart, arms at your sides.
- Inhale and exhale intentionally during the routine.
- Move your right foot out in front of you and slowly rotate your foot in a clockwise motion, keeping the ball of your foot on the floor. This will rotate your knee and hip joints, as well as stretch the ligaments and muscles in your right leg. Do at least five rotations.
- Repeat the rotation counterclockwise.
- Bring your feet together.
- Breathe in deeply. Exhale completely.

Repeat the movement, this time with your left foot extended.

•　　•　　•

You have made me stride freely, and my feet do not slip.
—2 Samuel 22:37

On Your Feet

On Your Back

On Your Stomach

Six Postures
of Prayer

Group Movement

Journal Pages

Stand with feet more than shoulder-width apart, arms stretched out to the sides, palms down.

- Bend forward, keeping back and knees straight, but do not lock your knees.
- Slowly reach down and place your right hand on the outside of your left shin. Keep your left arm straight out to the side.
- Pause and breathe in and out.
- As you inhale again, slide your right hand slowly down your shin as far as you are able.
- Raise your left hand upward toward the ceiling or sky. Hold that posture.

Option: As you are comfortable, rotate further to the left, turning your head and eyes to look up at your extended hand.

- As you exhale, slowly lower your left arm and raise yourself upward into a standing position.
- Breathe in deeply. Exhale completely.

Repeat the same movement, this time with the left hand on the right shin and right arm raised upward.

●　　●　　●

I will give you as a light to the nations, that my salvation may reach to the end of the earth.
—Isaiah 49:6

On Your Feet

On Your Back

On Your Stomach

Six Postures of Prayer

Group Movement

Journal Pages

Stand up straight with feet slightly apart, arms at your sides.

- If you are just beginning this movement, hold a short rope, necktie, belt, or rolled towel in your right hand.
- Inhale and exhale intentionally during the routine.
- Raise your right arm over your head, then bend your elbow, so your hand is at your shoulder.
- Reach your left hand behind your back, grasping for the object you were holding in your right hand. Take hold with your hands as close together as comfortable.

Option: As you are comfortable, forego using the object and clasp your fingers together.

- Alternate pulling down with your left arm and then pulling up with your right hand.
- With your left hand, release the object. Bring your arms back to your sides, allowing your arms to swing freely.
- Breathe in deeply. Exhale completely.

Repeat the same movement, this time starting with the left arm.

• • •

Ah Lord GOD! It is you who made the heavens and the earth by your great power and by your outstretched arm! Nothing is too hard for you.
—Jeremiah 32:17

Stand up straight with feet slightly more than shoulder-width apart, hands on your hips.

- Inhale and exhale intentionally during the routine.
- Slowly rotate your hips clockwise in a big circle, as if you were spinning a hula hoop.
- Following a few rotations, reverse the movement to counter-clockwise motions.
- Return to the first position.
- Breathe in deeply. Exhale completely.

●   ●   ●

"In God we live and move and have our being."
—*Acts 17:28 (NIV)*

On Your Feet

On Your Back

On Your Stomach

Six Postures of Prayer

Group Movement

Journal Pages

Stand up straight with feet slightly more than shoulder-width apart, arms at your side.

- Clasp your hands behind your back, locking your fingers.
- As you inhale, slowly bend forward, raising your arms behind you. Keep bending forward very slowly, as far as you are able. Bring your arms as far forward as you are able.
- As you exhale, slowly rise from this position.
- Stand up straight, releasing your hands and allowing your arms to swing freely.
- Breathe in deeply. Exhale completely.

●   ●   ●

I stretch out my hands to you; my soul thirsts for you.
—*Psalm 143:6*

Stand up straight with feet slightly more than shoulder-width apart, hands on your hips.

- Clasp your hands behind your back, locking your fingers.
- As you inhale, pull your arms behind you as far as you are able, bending backward and pushing your stomach forward.

Option: As you are comfortable, tip your head back.

- As you exhale, slowly return to an upright position.
- Stand up straight, releasing your hands and allowing your arms to swing freely.
- Breathe in deeply. Exhale completely.

● ● ●

Lift up your eyes to the heavens, and look at the earth beneath; . . . my salvation will be forever, and my deliverance will never be ended.
—*Isaiah 51:6*

On Your Feet

On Your Back

On Your Stomach

Six Postures of Prayer

Group Movement

Journal Pages

Stand up straight with feet slightly more than shoulder-width apart, arms hanging freely at your sides.

- Inhale and exhale intentionally during the routine.
- Slowly begin swinging your arms back and forth. Add the upper half of your body to the movement, bending forward slowly. With each back and forth motion, reach a bit lower for the floor.
- Try to touch the floor with your fingertips, or in time, your palms.
- Slowly rise up from the bent-over posture, continuing to sway back and forth until you are again upright.
- Breathe in deeply. Exhale completely.

Let peoples serve you, and nations bow down to you.
—Genesis 27:29

On Your Feet

On Your Back

On Your Stomach

Six Postures of Prayer

Group Movement

Journal Pages

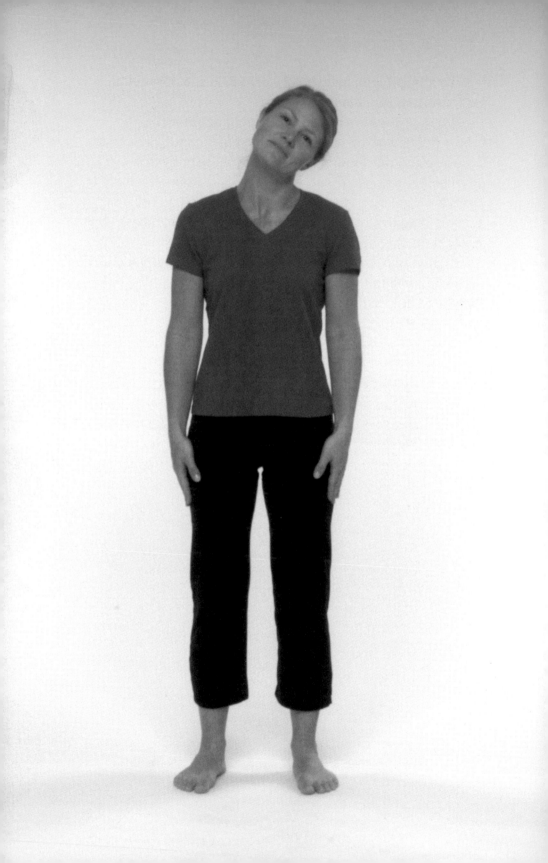

Stand up straight with feet slightly more than shoulder-width apart, hands on your hips.

- Inhale and exhale intentionally during the routine.
- Tilt your head to the left. Slowly move your head to the front, then to the right, loosening neck muscles through the stretching.
- From the right, repeat the same movement back to the left side. (It is not recommended to tilt your head to the back in doing this movement.)
- After a number of these motions, bring your head upright again.
- Breathe in deeply. Exhale completely.

● ● ●

Thus says God, the LORD, *who created the heavens and stretched them out, who spread out the earth and what comes from it, who gives breath to the people upon it and spirit to those who walk in it: "I am the* LORD, *I have called you in righteousness, I have taken you by the hand and kept you; I have given you as a covenant to the people, a light to the nations."*
—*Isaiah 42:5-6*

On Your Feet

On Your Back

On Your Stomach

Six Postures of Prayer

Group Movement

Journal Pages

Stand up straight with feet slightly more than shoulder-width apart.
- Raise your arms over your head.
- Inhale and exhale intentionally during the routine.
- Tilt the entire upper portion of your body to the left, bending from the waist.
- Slowly bring your upper body forward. As you bend, your arms should sweep from the left position forward and down toward the floor.
- From this position, bring your body up to the right, again sweeping your arms from the floor to the side.
- From the right, come back to the upright center position, then tilt left again. (It is not recommended to tilt your torso to the back in doing this movement.)
- After a number of these clockwise movements, reverse the motion to counter-clockwise and repeat for an equal amount of time.
- To end the movement, come center and inhale deeply.
- Exhale, allowing your arms to fall slowly to your sides.
- Breathe in deeply. Exhale completely.

● ● ●

You stretch out your hand to heal, and signs and wonders are performed through the name of your holy servant Jesus.
—*Acts 4:30*

Stand up straight with feet slightly more than shoulder-width apart, stretching out your arms to the sides, palms down.

- Inhale and exhale intentionally during this movement.
- Rotate your torso and hips to the left, bringing the left arm back as far as you are able. Then rotate to the right, leading with your right arm. This movement helps to align the back and spine.
- Continue the back and forth movement several times. Watch your fingers on the hand that is leading the movement, turning your head to see your hand at its farthest stretch behind you.
- To end the movement, come center and inhale deeply.
- Exhale, allowing your arms to fall slowly to your sides.
- Breathe in deeply. Exhale completely.

• • •

I keep the LORD always before me; because the Lord God is at my right hand, I shall not be moved. Therefore my heart is glad, and my soul rejoices; my body also rests secure.
—*Psalm 16:8-9 (NIV)*

On Your Feet

On Your Back

On Your Stomach

Six Postures of Prayer

Group Movement

Journal Pages

The Movements

Section Two:
On Your Back

Lie on your back on a mat or pad, arms at your side.

- Breathe in deeply. Exhale completely.
- As you next inhale, slowly bend your knees, then lift up your legs and roll your weight onto your shoulders.
- Support this posture by placing your hands behind your hips or back, with your elbows on the floor.
- Try to keep your legs as vertical as possible using your abdominal muscles to help you balance.
- Point your toes.
- Hold this position as you breathe out and in several times.
- Continue to the next movement.

Trust in the LORD with all your heart, and do not rely on your own insight. In all your ways acknowledge him, and he will make straight your paths. Do not be wise in your own eyes; fear the LORD, and turn away from evil. It will be a healing for your flesh and a refreshment for your body.
—*Proverbs 3:5-8*

This movement continues from the previous pose.
- Inhale deeply.
- As you exhale, slowly bend your right knee and bring it toward your face.
- As you inhale again, slowly raise your right leg.
- Repeat this same movement with your left leg, exhaling while bringing your left knee toward your face, inhaling while raising your left leg again.
- Repeat these knee bends several times.
- Come back to the original pose with both legs in a vertical position.
- Breathe in deeply. Exhale completely.
- Continue with the next movement.

● ● ●

I appeal to you therefore, brothers and sisters, by the mercies of God, to present your bodies as a living sacrifice, holy and acceptable to God, which is your spiritual worship.
—Romans 12:1

On Your Feet

On Your Back

On Your Stomach

Six Postures of Prayer

Group Movement

Journal Pages

This movement continues from the previous pose.
- Inhale deeply.
- As you exhale, slowly bend your knees and lower both legs. Both knees should be in front of your face.
- As you continue bending your legs into your body, release your hands from your hips. Allow your back to slowly roll down to the floor.
- Stretch your legs out . . . but hold your legs straight and slightly off the floor. Use your abdominal muscles to keep your feet raised. Place your hands under your head for support.
- Breathe in deeply. Exhale completely.
- Continue to the next movement.

I will give thanks to the LORD with my whole heart; I will tell of all your wonderful deeds.
—Psalm 9:1

On Your Feet

On Your Back

On Your Stomach

Six Postures of Prayer

Group Movement

Journal Pages

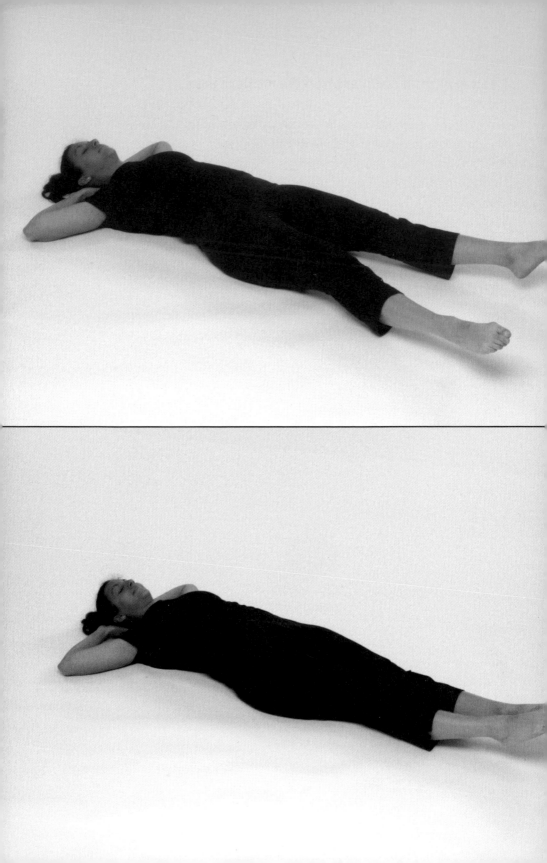

This movement continues from the previous pose.

- Inhale and exhale intentionally during this movement.
- While holding your legs straight and slightly off the floor, spread your legs wide apart and bring them back together a number of times. Try to keep your legs within several inches of the floor—not too high, but not touching the floor. Use your abdominal muscles and keep your back pressed firmly to the floor.
- Bring your feet together. Hold them off the floor as long as you are able.
- Lower your feet to the floor and relax your muscles.
- Breathe in deeply. Exhale completely.

The spirit of God has made me, and the breath of the Almighty gives me life.
—Job 33:4

On Your Feet

On Your Back

On Your Stomach

Six Postures of Prayer

Group Movement

Journal Pages

Lie on your back.

- Inhale and exhale intentionally during this movement.
- Stretch your arms above your head as far as you are able. Then clasp your hands together and bring them under your head.
- Raise your chin toward your chest, with your elbows out.
- Bend your knees and raise your legs. Bring your right knee toward your forehead as you straighten your left leg.
- Begin to do a series of slow, intentional movements as if riding a bicycle. Stretch your legs out as far as possible. Do not allow your feet to touch the floor.
- To end the movement, lower your head to the floor and bend both knees to your chest, stretching your lower back.
- Breathe in deeply. Exhale completely.
- Continue to the next movement.

● ● ●

Now, discipline always seems painful rather than pleasant at the time, but later it yields the peaceful fruit of righteousness to those who have been trained by it. Therefore lift your drooping hands and strengthen your weak knees, and make straight paths for your feet, so that what is lame may not be put out of joint, but rather be healed.
—Hebrews 12:11-13

On Your Feet

On Your Back

On Your Stomach

Six Postures of Prayer

Group Movement

Journal Pages

This movement continues from the previous pose.

- Inhale and exhale intentionally during this movement.
- Move your knees back to a central position, keeping your feet off the floor. Keep your hands folded behind your head and your chin tucked toward your chest.
- Do crunch movements. As you inhale, bring your left elbow across your body to touch the outside of your right knee.
- As you exhale, lower your shoulders back to the floor.
- Bring your right elbow to the outside of the left knee.
- Continue alternating sides, breathing in and out with each motion.
- Repeat these stomach crunches for as long as you wish or are able.
- When you are finished, slowly stretch your legs out and lower them to within a few inches of the floor. Hold them off the floor for several seconds, increasing the time as you continue these stretches.
- Breathe in deeply. Exhale completely.

●　　　●　　　●

Strengthen the weak hands, and make firm the feeble knees. Say to those who are of a fearful heart, "Be strong, do not fear! Here is your God."
—Isaiah 35:3-4

On Your Feet

On Your Back

On Your Stomach

Six Postures of Prayer

Group Movement

Journal Pages

Lie on your back.

- Stretch your arms out to each side in a cruciform position.
- Inhale and exhale intentionally during this movement.
- As you inhale, raise your right leg, keeping your knee straight and toes pointed.
- Pressing down on the floor with your hands, move your raised leg as far over to the left as you are able. The top portion of your body should remain flat on the floor, while the lower half rotates to the left.
- Hold the position for a few moments, then exhale and slowly reverse the movement, bringing your right leg back to the floor.
- Breathe in deeply. Exhale completely.

Repeat the movement again, this time using your left leg and rotating your lower body to the right.

He himself bore our sins in his body on the cross, so that, free from sins, we might live for righteousness; by his wounds you have been healed.
—1 Peter 2:24

On Your Feet

On Your Back

On Your Stomach

Six Postures of Prayer

Group Movement

Journal Pages

Lie on your back.

- Stretch your arms out to each side in a cruciform position.
- Bend your right knee, placing your right foot next to your left knee.
- As you inhale, tilt your right knee to the left as far as you are able.
- At the same time, move your left arm in the opposite direction, using your left hand to grasp your right elbow. The lower portion of your body will be rotating toward the left, while the top half is turning to the right.
- Exhale. Hold this position for a few moments, breathing in and out.
- Return to the original cruciform position.
- Breathe in deeply. Exhale completely.

Repeat the movement again, this time bending your left knee and rotating your lower body to the right while your right arm and torso move to the left.

•　　　•　　　•

For no one ever hates his own body, but he nourishes and tenderly cares for it, just as Christ does for the Church, because we are members of his body.
—Ephesians 5:29-30

On Your Feet

On Your Back

On Your Stomach

Six Postures of Prayer

Group Movement

Journal Pages

The Movements

Section Three:
On Your Stomach

Lie on your stomach on a mat or pad.

- Bend your elbows and place your palms on the floor near your shoulders. Place the tops of your feet against the floor and point your toes.
- Inhale as you slowly raise your torso with your arms. Your knees and lower legs will remain on the floor with your feet pointing back, allowing your body to arch in a crescent shape.

Option: As you become comfortable with this movement, tilt your head upward to look at the ceiling. Move your eyes in large clockwise circles as you look upward.

- Exhale and hold this posture, stretching the back.
- Inhale deeply and begin to slowly lower yourself back to the floor. Exhale as you reach the floor, resting your forehead on the ground.
- Breathe in deeply. Exhale completely.

Repeat the stretch. If you look up at the ceiling, this time rotate your eyes counterclockwise.

To you I lift up my eyes, O you who are enthroned in the heavens!
—Psalm 123:1

On Your Feet

On Your Back

On Your Stomach

Six Postures of Prayer

Group Movement

Journal Pages

Begin on your hands and knees, with your back parallel to the floor.

- The tops of your feet should be against the floor.
- As you inhale, slowly bend your head forward and arch your back upward in a cat-like stretch, pushing your hands into the floor. Hold the position for a moment.
- As you exhale, slowly lift your head upward and push your stomach toward the floor, reversing the curve of your back.
- Repeat the sequence twice more, drawing in as much air as you are able and expelling it through pressed lips.
- Continue to the next movement.

But then a hand touched me and roused me to my hands and knees.
—Daniel 10:10

On Your Feet

On Your Back

On Your Stomach

Six Postures of Prayer

Group Movement

Journal Pages

This movement continues from the previous pose.

- With hands still on the floor, turn your toes under and move onto your feet.
- Pressing down into the floor, bend at the waist and straighten your legs until you are in a triangle-like arch. Try to make your arms, your back, and your knees as straight as possible. Move your feet closer to your hands if necessary.
- Hold the posture, breathing in and out in regular sequences.
- Slowly bend your knees and return to the first position.
- Breathe in deeply. Exhale completely.

I bow down toward your holy temple and give thanks to your name for your steadfast love and your faithfulness; for you have exalted your name and your word above everything.
—Psalm 138:2

On Your Feet

On Your Back

On Your Stomach

Six Postures of Prayer

Group Movement

Journal Pages

Begin by standing upright.
- Inhale and exhale intentionally during the routine.
- Bending forward at the waist and knees, place your hands on the floor to provide balance.
- Carefully move your right leg back as far as you are able into a straddle position.
- Bend your left knee at a right angle to the floor, adjusting your back leg for the stretch. Be sure your left knee is behind or in line with your left ankle. To prevent injury, your knee should not be positioned farther forward than your ankle. Place your hands, one on top of the other on your left knee.

Option: In time, you may also wish to stretch your arms outward and upward.

- Balance in this position and inhale and exhale.
- Return your hands to the floor. Bring your left foot forward to meet your right.
- Stand up straight. Breathe in deeply. Exhale completely.

Repeat the stretch, this time moving your left leg back and bending your right knee in a right angle to the floor.

• • •

Therefore God also highly exalted him and gave him the name that is above every name, so that at the name of Jesus every knee should bend, in heaven and on earth and under the earth, and every tongue should confess that Jesus Christ is Lord, to the glory of God the Father.
—Philippians 2:9-11

The Movements

Section Four:
Six Postures
of Prayer

Adoration

Some people call this first posture "The Child" or "Child's Pose." It is an appropriate pose for a prayer of adoration.

Begin on your knees, sitting back on your heels, with the tops of your feet flat to the floor.

- While taking in a deep breath, raise your arms above your head.
- As you exhale, slowly lower your face toward the floor, folding forward from the hips. Stretch your arms out in front of you and place your hands flat on the floor.
- Offer the prayer of an adoring child, glorifying and offering thanksgiving to God.
- Breathe in deeply. Exhale completely.
- Continue to the next movement.

I love you, O LORD, my strength.
  —Psalm 18:1

On Your Feet

On Your Back

On Your Stomach

Six Postures of Prayer

Group Movement

Journal Pages

Confession

From the pose of adoration, inhale, raise up your head slightly, and bring your hands behind you, clasping your fingers together.

- As you exhale, lower your face toward the floor or to your knees and assume a posture that wraps you in a tight, bundled position.
- Breathe in deeply. Exhale completely.
- In this bound-up position, remember that we are in bondage to our human brokenness and sinful nature. Offer to our God of grace anything that separates you from God and from one another, asking for forgiveness and freedom from the brokenness of our human nature.
- Exhale as you let go of all that you confessed.
- Continue to the next movement.

If we confess our sins, God who is faithful and just will forgive us our sins and cleanse us from all unrighteousness.
—1 John 1:9 (NIV)

On Your Feet

On Your Back

On Your Stomach

Six Postures of Prayer

Group Movement

Journal Pages

Absolution

From the pose of confession, exhale as you release your hands from the bonded position. Raise the upper half of your body so that you are sitting on your heels, with your toes turned under.

- As you inhale, stretch your hands and arms upward and over your head as far as you are able. Reach upward to touch the fingertips of a gracious God who reaches out with love, compassion, and absolution.
- Breathe while holding the position momentarily, enjoying the cleansing of the One who promises to "remember our sin no more."
- Breathe in deeply. As you exhale, slowly lower your arms, keeping them straight on the way down. Experience the grace and love of God showering over you.
- Bring your hands together onto your lap and bow your head. Bask in the joy of forgiveness.
- Breathe in deeply. Exhale completely.
- Continue to the next movement.

●   ●   ●

Then I acknowledged my sin to you, and I did not hide my iniquity; I said, "I will confess my transgressions to the LORD," and you forgave the guilt of my sin.
—Psalm 32:5

On Your Feet

On Your Back

On Your Stomach

Six Postures of Prayer

Group Movement

Journal Pages

Petition

From the pose of absolution, still sitting on your heels with your back straight and upright, raise your head.

- Place your right hand on your left shoulder, and cross your left hand over to your right shoulder.
- With arms folded and cross-shaped over your heart, offer prayers of personal petition for the needs you have in your own heart.

Some suggestions: Pray for wisdom and discernment in the choices you will make this day. Pray for courage in your faith-walk and witness. Pray for well-chosen words and a heart filled with grace and love for God and one another.

- Breathe in deeply. Exhale completely.
- Continue to the next movement.

● ● ●

[Daniel] continued to go to his house . . . and to get down on his knees three times a day to pray to his God and praise him.
—Daniel 6:10

On Your Feet

On Your Back

On Your Stomach

Six Postures of Prayer

Group Movement

Journal Pages

Intercession

From the pose of petition, change your position to sit directly on the floor with your feet in front of you.

- Bend your knees and put your heels together. Fold your hands and cup them around your toes. Pull your feet in as close to your body as you are able.
- Offer prayers of intercession for others—family members, friends, leaders in your faith community, co-workers, and all others on your prayer list.
- If it does not become a distraction for your intercessory prayers, slowly move your knees up and down to further stretch the upper legs and thighs.
- Breathe in deeply. Exhale completely.
- Continue to the next movement.

● ● ●

First of all, then, I urge that supplications, prayers, intercessions, and thanksgivings be made for everyone.
—1 Timothy 2:1

On Your Feet

On Your Back

On Your Stomach

Six Postures of Prayer

Group Movement

Journal Pages

Contemplation

From the pose of intercession, change your position slightly by crossing your legs.

Option: As you are comfortable and gain flexibility, move your legs tighter together, resting your ankles on top of your calves.

- Sit up tall with your back straight. Place your hands on your knees in a receiving position, palms open and turned upward, or put them together in a prayer position in front of your heart.
- Draw in a deep breath and hold it.
- Slowly exhale. Repeat this breathing pattern throughout this time of prayer.
- This universal posture of contemplation invites the person of prayer to receive rather than to offer. It is a time of listening rather than asking or speaking. Listen to the inner voice of God and the leading of the Spirit. Relax in this position and rest in the presence of God.
- Breathe slowly, intentionally. Listen carefully.

This completes the individual stretches, postures, and movements. Take a final deep breath and exhale as you extinguish your candle.

●   ●   ●

Be still, and know that I am God! I am exalted among the nations, I am exalted in the earth.
—Psalm 46:10

On Your Feet

On Your Back

On Your Stomach

Six Postures of Prayer

Group Movement

Journal Pages

The Movements

Section Five:
Group Movement

Light a candle and place it in the center of the room.
Form a circle around the candle.

• Altogether, take three small steps forward into the circle toward the center. As you do so, inhale and lift up your hands, turning your palms upward to offer a prayer to God.
• As you exhale, slowly lower your hands to your sides and take three steps backward.
• Repeat the movement several times.
• At the end of this routine, extinguish and remove the candle.
• Invite anyone so willing into the center of your sacred circle.
• Stretch your hands and arms over the person and pray with and for them.

On Your Feet

On Your Back

On Your Stomach

Six Postures
of Prayer

Group Movement

Journal Pages

Stretch and Pray

Section Six:
Journal Pages

Devotional Thought

As I begin this holy time, I stretch my hands upward toward my Creator, receiving in body, soul, and mind God's love and presence during these sacred moments.

Let us lift up our hearts as well as our hands to God in heaven.
—Lamentations 3:41

This devotional thought especially connects to the movement on page 2.

Date _____

_____

_____

_____

_____

_____

_____

_____

_____

_____

_____

_____

_____

Devotional Thought

What is one way that I will lean into the grace of God this day?

To you, O LORD, I lift up my soul.
—Psalm 25:1

This devotional thought especially connects to the movement on page 4.

Date _____

_____

_____

_____

_____

_____

_____

_____

_____

_____

_____

_____

_____

On Your Feet

On Your Back

On Your Stomach

Six Postures of Prayer

Group Movement

Journal Pages

Devotional Thought
How do I experience the arms of God's embrace?

She girds herself with strength, and makes her arms strong.
—Proverbs 31:17

This devotional thought especially connects to the movement on page 6.

Date _____

_____

_____

_____

_____

_____

_____

_____

_____

_____

_____

_____

_____

Devotional Thought

I am thankful for the opportunities to be near to the Holy One who has given me life, and who walks side-by-side with me each day.

You have made me stride freely, and my feet do not slip.
—2 Samuel 22:37

This devotional thought especially connects to the movement on page 8.

Date _____

_____

_____

_____

_____

_____

_____

_____

_____

_____

_____

_____

_____

_____

On Your Feet

On Your Back

On Your Stomach

Six Postures of Prayer

Group Movement

Journal Pages

Devotional Thought

God reaches long, outstretched arms to me this day, allowing me to reflect God's light and share God's gifts to another.

I will give you as a light to the nations, that my salvation may reach to the end of the earth.
—Isaiah 49:6

This devotional thought especially connects to the movement on page 10.

Date _____

_____

_____

_____

_____

_____

_____

_____

_____

_____

_____

_____

_____

Devotional Thought

The strength and possibilities of God meet me where I am often weak and incapable. I am made strong in my weakness by the might of God.

Ah Lord GOD! It is you who made the heavens and the earth by your great power and by your outstretched arm! Nothing is too hard for you.
—*Jeremiah 32:17*

This devotional thought especially connects to the movement on page 12.

Date _____

_____

_____

_____

_____

_____

_____

_____

_____

_____

_____

_____

On Your Feet

On Your Back

On Your Stomach

Six Postures of Prayer

Group Movement

Journal Pages

Devotional Thought

I give thanks that God offers me the strength and will to move, to stretch, to breathe, to be strengthened, to seek wellness, and to know daily joy.

"In God we live and move and have our being."
—*Acts 17:28 (NIV)*

This devotional thought especially connects to the movement on page 14.

Date _____

_____

_____

_____

_____

_____

_____

_____

_____

_____

_____

_____

Devotional Thought

As I face my life, I am humbled some moments and exalted in others. What is it that humbles me before God?

I stretch out my hands to you; my soul thirsts for you.
—Psalm 143:6

This devotional thought especially connects to the movement on page 16.

Date _____

On Your Feet

On Your Back

On Your Stomach

Six Postures of Prayer

Group Movement

Journal Pages

Devotional Thought

As I face my life, I am humbled some moments and exalted in others. How is it that God exalts me?

Lift up your eyes to the heavens, and look at the earth beneath; . . . my salvation will be forever, and my deliverance will never be ended.
—Isaiah 51:6

This devotional thought especially connects to the movement on page 18.

Date _____

_____

_____

_____

_____

_____

_____

_____

_____

_____

_____

_____

Devotional Thought

What is it about God that brings forth my deepest devotion, reverence, and humble prayers of thanksgiving and praise?

Let peoples serve you, and nations bow down to you.
—Genesis 27:29

This devotional thought especially connects to the movement on page 20.

Date _____

_____

_____

_____

_____

_____

_____

_____

_____

_____

_____

_____

On Your Feet

On Your Back

On Your Stomach

Six Postures of Prayer

Group Movement

Journal Pages

Devotional Thought

How do I sense the breath of God in my being, my living, and my faith?

Thus says God, the LORD, who created the heavens and stretched them out, who spread out the earth and what comes from it, who gives breath to the people upon it and spirit to those who walk in it: "I am the LORD, I have called you in righteousness, I have taken you by the hand and kept you; I have given you as a covenant to the people, a light to the nations."
—Isaiah 42:5-6

This devotional thought especially connects to the movement on page 22.

Date _____

_____

_____

_____

_____

_____

_____

_____

_____

_____

_____

_____

Devotional Thought

As God stretches hands of healing over me, what signs and wonders of God am I aware of at this time in my life?

You stretch out your hand to heal, and signs and wonders are performed through the name of your holy servant Jesus.
—Acts 4:30

This devotional thought especially connects to the movement on page 24.

Date _____

_____

_____

_____

_____

_____

_____

_____

_____

_____

_____

_____

_____

_____

On Your Feet

On Your Back

On Your Stomach

Six Postures of Prayer

Group Movement

Journal Pages

Devotional Thought

I am thankful for the parts of my being that are healthy, and I pray for that which seeks renewal and wholeness.

I keep the LORD always before me; because the Lord God is at my right hand, I shall not be moved. Therefore my heart is glad, and my soul rejoices; my body also rests secure.
—Psalm 16:8-9 (NIV)

This devotional thought especially connects to the movement on page 26.

Date _____

_____

_____

_____

_____

_____

_____

_____

_____

_____

_____

_____

Devotional Thought

Knowing the promises and presence of God, what situations lie before me where I will trust in my Lord God with all my heart, with all my being?

Trust in the LORD with all your heart, and do not rely on your own insight. In all your ways acknowledge him, and he will make straight your paths. Do not be wise in your own eyes; fear the LORD, and turn away from evil. It will be a healing for your flesh and a refreshment for your body.
—Proverbs 3:5-8

This devotional thought especially connects to the movement on page 30.

Date _____

_____

_____

_____

_____

_____

_____

_____

_____

_____

_____

On Your Feet

On Your Back

On Your Stomach

Six Postures of Prayer

Group Movement

Journal Pages

Devotional Thought

How do I acknowledge God with my life and my being in what I say and do?

I appeal to you therefore, brothers and sisters, by the mercies of God, to present your bodies as a living sacrifice, holy and acceptable to God, which is your spiritual worship.
—Romans 12:1

This devotional thought especially connects to the movement on page 32.

Date _____

_____

_____

_____

_____

_____

_____

_____

_____

_____

_____

_____

Devotional Thought

For what specific reasons do I give thanks for God's healing hand and renewing Spirit?

I will give thanks to the LORD with my whole heart; I will tell of all your wonderful deeds.
—Psalm 9:1

This devotional thought especially connects to the movement on page 34.

Date _____

_____

_____

_____

_____

_____

_____

_____

_____

_____

_____

_____

On Your Feet

On Your Back

On Your Stomach

Six Postures of Prayer

Group Movement

Journal Pages

Devotional Thought

Each movement I make, each breath I take is a gift of miraculous proportions. In me, God has created an intricate and complex creature.

The spirit of God has made me, and the breath of the Almighty gives me life.
—*Job 33:4*

This devotional thought especially connects to the movement on page 36.

Date _____

_____

_____

_____

_____

_____

_____

_____

_____

_____

_____

_____

Devotional Thought

I am aware that my body, mind, heart, and soul are interconnected. When one part hurts, all other parts suffer. When one part is strengthened, my whole self is renewed.

Now, discipline always seems painful rather than pleasant at the time, but later it yields the peaceful fruit of righteousness to those who have been trained by it. Therefore lift your drooping hands and strengthen your weak knees, and make straight paths for your feet, so that what is lame may not be put out of joint, but rather be healed.
—Hebrews 12:11-13

This devotional thought especially connects to the movement on page 38.

Date _____

_____

_____

_____

_____

_____

_____

_____

_____

_____

On Your Feet

On Your Back

On Your Stomach

Six Postures of Prayer

Group Movement

Journal Pages

Devotional Thought

Wellness is wholistic. Today, I thank God for the various parts of my being that all together make me who I am as a child of God and a citizen of God's creation.

Strengthen the weak hands, and make firm the feeble knees. Say to those who are of a fearful heart, "Be strong, do not fear! Here is your God."
—Isaiah 35:3-4

This devotional thought especially connects to the movement on page 40.

Date _____

_____

_____

_____

_____

_____

_____

_____

_____

_____

_____

_____

Devotional Thought

As I assume the position my Savior assumed for me, I reflect on how I have been made strong in his weakness, set free, and healed.

He himself bore our sins in his body on the cross, so that, free from sins, we might live for righteousness; by his wounds you have been healed.
—1 Peter 2:24

This devotional thought especially connects to the movement on page 42.

Date _____

_____

_____

_____

_____

_____

_____

_____

_____

_____

_____

On Your Feet

On Your Back

On Your Stomach

Six Postures of Prayer

Group Movement

Journal Pages

Devotional Thought

What part of me is most symbolic of my place in the body of Christ? I pray for both my physical and spiritual dimensions.

For no one ever hates his own body, but he nourishes and tenderly cares for it, just as Christ does for the Church, because we are members of his body.
—Ephesians 5:29-30

This devotional thought especially connects to the movement on page 44.

Date _____

_____

_____

_____

_____

_____

_____

_____

_____

_____

_____

Devotional Thought

For what part of life that I see or sense am I most thankful?

To you I lift up my eyes, O you who are enthroned in the heavens!
—Psalm 123:1

This devotional thought especially connects to the movement on page 48.

Date _____

_____

_____

_____

_____

_____

_____

_____

_____

_____

_____

_____

On Your Feet

On Your Back

On Your Stomach

Six Postures
of Prayer

Group Movement

Journal Pages

Devotional Thought

Deep breathing; long, careful stretching; deep believing; full, intentional praying fill me with the wonders of God. How will I enjoy these disciplines and opportunities today?

But then a hand touched me and roused me to my hands and knees.
—Daniel 10:10

This devotional thought especially connects to the movement on page 50.

Date _____

_____

_____

_____

_____

_____

_____

_____

_____

_____

_____

_____

Devotional Thought

Many faiths express their devotion with specific body movements and postures. Today I will focus on actions or positions that express my worship.

I bow down toward your holy temple and give thanks to your name for your steadfast love and your faithfulness; for you have exalted your name and your word above everything.
—Psalm 138:2

This devotional thought especially connects to the movement on page 52.

Date _____

_____

_____

_____

_____

_____

_____

_____

_____

_____

_____

On Your Feet

On Your Back

On Your Stomach

Six Postures of Prayer

Group Movement

Journal Pages

Devotional Thought

God calls me to the center of God's own being through reverence, prayer, devotional reading, listening, and even focused movement and meaningful posturing. Upon what thought or activity is God centering me this day?

Therefore God also highly exalted him and gave him the name that is above every name, so that at the name of Jesus every knee should bend, in heaven and on earth and under the earth, and every tongue should confess that Jesus Christ is Lord, to the glory of God the Father.
—Philippians 2:9-11

This devotional thought especially connects to the movement on page 54.

Date _____

_____

_____

_____

_____

_____

_____

_____

_____

_____

_____

Devotional Thought

I offer praise to God in prayers expressing my love and devotion.

I love you, O LORD, my strength.
—Psalm 18:1

This devotional thought especially connects to the movement on page 58.

Date _____

_____

_____

_____

_____

_____

_____

_____

_____

_____

_____

_____

_____

On Your Feet

On Your Back

On Your Stomach

Six Postures
of Prayer

Group Movement

Journal Pages

Devotional Thought

As I confess brokenness and imperfection, I admit my errors, ask for forgiveness and undeserved grace, and pray for a new beginning.

If we confess our sins, God who is faithful and just will forgive us our sins and cleanse us from all unrighteousness.
—*1 John 1:9 (NIV)*

This devotional thought especially connects to the movement on page 60.

Date _____

_____

_____

_____

_____

_____

_____

_____

_____

_____

_____

_____

_____

Devotional Thought

I am freely offered the unconditional love of God, who takes away all that separates me from God and others. I pray for a heart open to this gracious gift.

Then I acknowledged my sin to you, and I did not hide my iniquity; I said, "I will confess my transgressions to the LORD," and you forgave the guilt of my sin.
—Psalm 32:5

This devotional thought especially connects to the movement on page 62.

Date _____

_____

_____

_____

_____

_____

_____

_____

_____

_____

_____

On Your Feet

On Your Back

On Your Stomach

Six Postures of Prayer

Group Movement

Journal Pages

Devotional Thought

God's own voice encourages me to call in times of need as well as thanksgiving. I offer my personal petition this day.

[Daniel] continued to go to his house . . . and to get down on his knees three times a day to pray to his God and praise him.
—*Daniel 6:10*

This devotional thought especially connects to the movement on page 64.

Date _____

_____

_____

_____

_____

_____

_____

_____

_____

_____

_____

_____

_____

_____

Devotional Thought

It is a privilege to pray for others, interceding to God on behalf of those in need, those I love, those for whom I seek God's care and presence.

First of all, then, I urge that supplications, prayers, intercessions, and thanksgivings be made for everyone.
—1 Timothy 2:1

This devotional thought especially connects to the movement on page 66.

Date _____

_____

_____

_____

_____

_____

_____

_____

_____

_____

_____

_____

On Your Feet

On Your Back

On Your Stomach

Six Postures of Prayer

Group Movement

Journal Pages

Devotional Thought
God promises to be present with me always, to the end of time. I wait in that presence, open, receptive, quiet, listening, and filled with expectation, wonder, and awe.

Be still, and know that I am God! I am exalted among the nations, I am exalted in the earth.
—Psalm 46:10

This devotional thought especially connects to the movement on page 68.

Date _____

_____

_____

_____

_____

_____

_____

_____

_____

_____

_____

_____

Other Resources from Augsburg Books

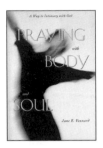

Praying with Body and Soul by Jane E. Vennard
144 pages, 0-8066-3614-9

Praying with Body and Soul involves the whole person: our senses, our bodies at rest or in motion, our imaginations, as well as our minds and emotions. By paying prayerful attention to the body, people will not only recognize the ways in which they already pray, but will learn how to deepen their relationship with God.

How to Keep a Spiritual Journal by Ron Klug
144 pages, 0-8066-4357-9

An indispensable guide that shows new ways to care for your soul with prayer, spiritual readings, and journal exercises. This book will help you understand your spiritual journey.

Emotional Wisdom by Robert Maclennan
96 pages, 0-8066-5140-7

Maclennan leads the reader in a spiritual exploration of human emotions. Each of the forty-four meditations begins with a biblical quotation; moves into a reflection on an emotion's purpose, expression, and metaphorical connection with nature; and finishes with thoughtful questions for reflection.

Making Room for God by Melvyn Matthews
96 pages, 0-8066-5159-8

Making Room for God encourages readers to increase their awareness of God by becoming more conscious of the value of their inner life. Each chapter contains simple exercises designed to transform the reader's prayer life and love for others.

Available wherever books are sold.